perspectives
ON DESIGN
CHICAGO

Published by

PANACHE
PANACHE PARTNERS

Panache Partners, LLC
1424 Gables Court
Plano, TX 75075
469.246.6060
Fax: 469.246.6062
www.panache.com

Publishers: Brian G. Carabet and John A. Shand

Printed in Malaysia

Distributed by Independent Publishers Group
800.888.4741

PUBLISHER'S DATA

Perspectives on Design Chicago

Library of Congress Control Number: 2010928693

ISBN 13: 978-1-933415-58-1
ISBN 10: 1-933415-58-4

First Printing 2010

10 9 8 7 6 5 4 3 2 1

Right: Scott Byron & Company, page 157

Previous Page: Eifler & Associates, page 19

Panache Partners, LLC, is dedicated to the restoration and
conservation of the environment. Our books are manufactured
with strict adherence to an environmental management system in
accordance with ISO 14001 standards, including the use of paper
from mills certified to derive their products from well-managed
forests. We are committed to continued investigation of alternative
paper products and environmentally responsible manufacturing
processes to ensure the preservation of our fragile planet.

perspectives
ON DESIGN
CHICAGO

introduction

Florian Architects, page 29

Creating the spaces in which we live and achieving the beauty we desire can be a daunting quest—a quest that is as diverse as each of our unique personalities. For some, it may be a serene, sculptural pool in the backyard; for others it may be an authentic Japanese tea house or a modernist space with Art Deco elements. Aspiring chefs may find a kitchen integrating the latest technology with classic materials their true sanctuary.

Perspectives on Design Chicago is a pictorial journey from conceptualizing your dream home to putting together the finishing touches to creating an outdoor oasis. Alongside the phenomenal photography, you will have a rare insight into how these tastemakers achieve such works of art and be inspired by their personal perspectives on design.

Within these pages, many fine artisans will share their wisdom, experience, and talent. It is the collaboration between these visionaries and the outstanding pride and craftsmanship of the products showcased that together achieve the remarkable. Learn from leaders in design about the aesthetics of a finely crafted stained glass window, how appropriate lighting can dramatically change the appearance of a landscape, or what is necessary to create a realistic mural that transports you to another place.

Whether your dream is to have a new home or one that has been redesigned to suit your lifestyle, *Perspectives on Design Chicago* will be both an enjoyable journey and a source of motivation.

Atelier Lapchi, page 133

contents

New Metal Crafts, page 145

"A house should reflect the uniqueness of its residents. As a project evolves and the architect-owner relationship grows, we can express this aspect more fully."

—Margaret McCurry

"Each home should be a unique expression of the people who dwell within its walls."

—Fred Wilson

New Metal Crafts, page 145

Michael E Breseman Architects, Ltd., page 49

Larry Zgoda Studio, page 97

Night Light, Inc., Landscape Illumination, page 179

"By designing an entry in human scale, a sense of delight is revealed and made more powerful as one steps inside the grand space."

—Michael E. Breseman

"Ordinary architectural prose can be elevated to poetry through carefully developed arrangement and finish."

—Tom Beeby

Morgante Wilson Architects, page 59

Wujcik Construction Group, Inc., page 79

Builders Ironworks, Inc., page 109

Signature Mural & Finish, page 151

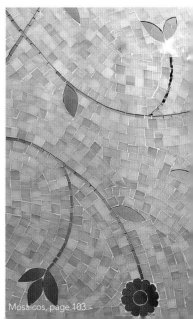
Mosaicos, page 103

Hammond Beeby Rupert Ainge, page 39

Michael E. Breseman Architects, Ltd., page 49

the concept

Architect John Eifler, FAIA, has known his passion since childhood. John founded his namesake firm in 1990 after nearly a decade at Skidmore, Owings and Merrill. While at SOM, John was largely responsible for the restoration of The James Charnley House, an 1892 Adler, Louis Sullivan, and Frank Lloyd Wright residential wonder on Chicago's Gold Coast. John has developed a reputation for being adept at beautifully restoring historic homes throughout America, most recently involved with Taliesin and Taliesin West for the Frank Lloyd Wright Foundation. Today, Eifler & Associates concentrates on achieving a balance of both new design and historic restoration projects, enjoying a variety of commercial, institutional, and residential work.

Trained as a modernist, he has studied the works of Wright, Alvar Aalto, and genius architects from the Bauhaus movement. Composition, form, choice materials, sculptural qualities, and a keen awareness of site are characteristic of his contemporary residential designs. John and his team thoughtfully develop interior design aspects as well: furniture, cabinetry, lighting, built-in millwork, and period kitchen elements to unify the exterior building elements with indoor living spaces. John's holistic approach to design is the firm's hallmark, a philosophy that pays homage to those who have gone before him.

"A design concept can be inspired by nature, an architectural vernacular, or historical precedent."

—John Eifler

EIFLER & ASSOCIATES

"Using indigenous materials not only reflects the region, it creates a visual vocabulary."

—John Eifler

ABOVE, FACING PAGE & PREVIOUS PAGES: We designed a modern interpretation of the quintessential lakeside cottage based on historical precedents incorporating natural wood, a sheltering roof, exterior terraces, and access to Lake Michigan. Our philosophy is to choose native materials whenever possible; the contemporary cottage design features local stone and cedar. An extensive use of glass allows for generous lake and sky views, as well as ease of access to the lakeside property through multiple doors and windows. We designed an expansive terrace to offer alfresco entertaining and recreation areas. The interior of the living space, with its fireplace and furniture, creates a cabin campgrounds ambience, where a cozy fire is the central element. Radiant-heated polished concrete floors stay warm during winter, while custom-fabricated furniture provides comfortable fireside seating. We designed the glass-enclosed master bedroom with its own fireplace; it has breathtaking lake vistas bringing the outdoors in.
Photographs by William Kildow

"Preserving the integrity of historic architecture is paramount, but we must make it functional for today's lifestyles."

—John Eifler

RIGHT: Our mission was to contemporize a kitchen with historical Newport roots. We maintained the authentic character of the house, while specifying new appliances, cabinets, and work surfaces for ultimate function. The La Cornue professional range in the period kitchen reflects the home's true original character. We commissioned handmade crackle-glazed tile in a rich, ochre color for the stove surround to mirror nature's mossy color tones.

FACING PAGE: We restored a circa-1917 Newport, Rhode Island, cottage to take advantage of its dramatic oceanside location with endless views. The project included extensive redesign and restoration of the terrace, sunroom, balcony, chimneys, windows, exterior stucco, and slate roof. We transformed a traditionally formal garden off the terrace into a wonderful, perennial cutting garden for the owners. Our objective to maintain the original historic character of the exterior façade and outdoor areas while providing updated interior spaces for the everyday needs of contemporary family life was successfully achieved.
Photographs by John Eifler

"To seamlessly integrate structures within the natural environment is true art."

—John Eifler

ABOVE & FACING PAGE: An entry view of the residence shows extensive use of glass for optimal vistas of the heavily wooded site in Oak Brook. We thoughtfully designed the huge exterior deck to preserve mature hickory and old oak trees, while creating a treehouse effect. Our firm follows the revered philosophy that a building's architectural design should develop out of its natural surroundings.
Photographs by William Kildow

"Good residential design can masterfully bring the outdoors in."

—John Eifler

ABOVE & FACING PAGE: Our clients are voracious readers, so we designed the master bedroom to incorporate a shared sitting room as a defined space for reading books and enjoying views of the tranquil forest while being warmed by the limestone fireplace. Walls are lined with cedar and fir, and warm-hued floors are maple hardwoods. The home's dining room is a very tall, open space for entertaining, set between two walls of glass to evoke an atmosphere of being outdoors. We planned the breakfast room as a smaller, intimate space specially designed for family meals; it intentionally faces east to receive morning sunlight.
Photographs by William Kildow

Florian Architects' philosophy underscores the concept that architecture is a communicative art in which true collaboration and stylistic diversity are paramount. Each residence the firm designs must meet exacting standards.

Chicago is one of the greatest architectural cities in the world and inspiration is everywhere, from Frank Lloyd Wright dwellings to skyscrapers designed by Mies van der Rohe and Louis Sullivan. Founded by Paul Florian, FAIA, Florian Architects lives up to its fair city's reputation for producing some of the most fascinating structures of all time. To create a residence of distinction, Paul believes that a house must embody the spirit of his clients; he personally guides the creative process. His award-winning firm has also gained notoriety in the design of national retail stores and avant-garde exhibitions, as well as original furniture and objects. As a renaissance man in the world of architectural and interior design, Paul has shared his passion and knowledge as a design instructor at major universities. His inspired designs are integral to the rich architectural fabric of the Windy City and its environs.

"A new home must complement rather than intrude—it should feel inevitable and timeless, an integral part of an existing community."

—Paul Florian

FLORIAN ARCHITECTS

"Environments should tell a story by providing a meaningful sequence of spaces and elements that engage and delight as they unfold."

—Paul Florian

TOP RIGHT: A limestone portico graces the informal mudroom entry. The arches of an outdoor porch frame wonderful views of the lake.

BOTTOM RIGHT: High baseboards, deep crown moulding, and oak flooring laid in a Versailles pattern create an intimate elegance in the dining room. Furnishings by Soucie Horner, Ltd.

FACING PAGE: The imposing double-height entry hall features full wainscoting; random-width oak floors are bordered by insets of mahogany. Although a single traditional architecture creates an integrated ambience inside the house, variation within this style enriches the sense of sequence and the character of individual spaces throughout. Movement from public to private spaces, from formal to informal, is articulated by shifts in levels and ceiling heights, materials, and different types of moulding. Subtle variations of traditional architectural elements bring the unexpected to each distinct room.

PREVIOUS PAGES: We are well versed in traditional styles. The English country houses of Sir Edwin Lutyens and his Edwardian contemporaries inspired our new home on a bluff overlooking Lake Michigan. The wooded triangular site presented challenges. We positioned the house to create a formal approach to the main entry, to preserve a stand of historic oaks, and to maximize lakefront views. The juxtaposition of hipped roofs and dormers to classical Georgian elements like Palladian windows, brick pilasters, and limestone porticos gives the building a sense of history, of being built over a long period of time. Although symmetrical wings enhance its formality, the front façade is softened by its materials: cream brick, buff-colored stone details, copper elements, stained mahogany doors, and natural slate paving and roof exude warmth. Furnishings by Soucie Horner, Ltd.
Photographs by Mark Heffron

"A home is a fine portrait that expresses the character of its owners and enhances their way of living."

—Paul Florian

RIGHT: The homeowners are sophisticated collectors of works by prominent American artists; this elegant living room provides ample space for a beautiful display of paintings acquired over the years. Higher ceilings created by a change in level with formal crown mouldings and strategically placed recessed lighting evoke a museum-inspired setting of casual luxury. Antique appointments and custom interior furnishings by Soucie Horner, Ltd.
Photograph by Mark Heffron

"We believe in close collaboration to better express a highly personal aesthetic, a unique vision."

—Paul Florian

LEFT: A dressing area lit by penthouse windows adjacent to the master bedroom overlooks the soaring dining room space below. The architecture was inspired by the owner's fascination with the decorative aspects of Modernism, including the designs of French Modernists Robert Mallet-Stevens and Le Corbusier as well as Chicago artist and designer Edgar Miller. Interlocking double-height spaces and industrial metal windows give the house an ambience reminiscent of a quintessential French artist's garret.

FACING PAGE: Custom metal windows set into a single pocket and curved plaster walls with minimal details provide a sculptural environment for the owner's collection of art and furniture. Bleached hickory flooring lends airy warmth to the space. The random tile pattern of the hearth recalls the work of Edgar Miller and other artists in the adjacent neighborhood. Dramatic renovation transformed a conventional brownstone on Burton Place into a chic, light-filled urban dwelling in keeping with its 1930s and '40s artisan-designed neighbors. We incorporated five levels including a roof garden; only bronze fireplaces, metal handrails, and a few walls and floors of the original structure remain. Furnishings by John Mark Horton.
Photographs by Michelle Litvin

"Interior architecture is exciting when the design has plasticity—curved volumes and glowing recesses give a sculptural quality to the space."

—Paul Florian

ABOVE: In the second-floor sitting room, the interior architecture synthesizes the simplicity of Modernism with the glamour of Art Deco. An integrated daybed and tiled end table are built into an alcove; curves add movement to the composition of plaster volumes.

FACING PAGE: Asymmetrical patterns of ribbed and etched glass panes set into a network of black metal window frames become functional works of art, admitting light as they screen views of adjacent buildings. Furnishings by John Mark Horton.
Photographs by Michelle Litvin

James Wright Hammond founded the firm in Chicago in 1961 on the premise that interaction between client and architect at all stages of the design and construction process produces the best buildings. Today, Thomas Beeby, FAIA—former Dean of the Yale School of Architecture—and his partners Dennis Rupert, FAIA, and Gary Ainge, AIA, continue the tradition of a design approach based on collaboration. With a diverse portfolio of work in institutional, educational, liturgical, and residential architecture, the partners have expanded their range nationally beyond the Chicago area.

Neutral in taste, style, and preference, the firm responds to the specific requirements of each project's site and context, which it attempts to reconcile with the individual needs and wants of each client. New designs and details therefore take their surroundings as a primary point of departure; these often extend recognizable architectural styles or blend styles to create a hybrid. Carefully considered details achieve seamless stylistic continuity throughout and emphasize each project as a unique response to a particular set of challenges.

"The serious study of old buildings can lead to an architecture of lasting quality."

—Tom Beeby

HAMMOND BEEBY RUPERT AINGE

"Authentic detail and genuine artifacts support each other in a meaningful dialogue."

—Tom Beeby

ABOVE LEFT: Flanked by matching basins and enclosures for the shower and water closet, the bathtub in the master bathroom is surrounded by a mirror-lined canopy, a focal element that adds depth to the room. Onyx is used throughout for the flooring and wainscoting; the cabinetry features custom French millwork.

ABOVE RIGHT & FACING PAGE: Comprising a suite for formal entertaining, the living and dining rooms are arranged along one side of the stair gallery. Windows located at the edges of the dining room reinforce the central placement of the table while in the living room lighting fixtures, furnishings, and hand-carved wall medallions in the style of Louis XV contrast with the restrained classicism of the panel mouldings and door trim. A clear sightline is maintained throughout, and complementary mirrors and chandeliers placed along this line establish the living and dining rooms as a linked pair.

PREVIOUS PAGES LEFT: An oblong gallery with a suspended stair at one end occupies a middle zone between the entrance foyer and the rooms for formal entertaining. The hall's pure geometry and its axially and symmetrically arranged door and window openings exhibit the strict geometry of 18th-century French Neoclassicism, which is softened by the curves of the stair, its balustrade, and the ornamental metalwork of the chandelier and paired wall sconces.

PREVIOUS PAGES RIGHT: On a site full of large coniferous trees, the house's design was inspired by the small châteaux built for members of the French court during the 18th century in the neighborhood of Versailles. Its division into three pavilions separates formal rooms for entertaining from informal living rooms and shapes exterior spaces—like the entry courtyard—as outdoor rooms.
Photographs by John Hall

"Ordinary architectural prose can be elevated to poetry through carefully developed arrangement and finish."

—Tom Beeby

ABOVE: An existing duplex was transformed into a two-story, wood-frame house planned throughout according to a four-inch module that left little margin for error, almost like an enlarged work of cabinetry. Precise use of natural materials responded to the site's context and the owner's interest in Asian art. Exposed exterior framing in Douglas fir reveals the major living spaces along one side of the house, with stone fireplaces at each end, and the lateral walls that separate these spaces form a zone of circulation. Large bronze-clad windows and a covered patio space frame spectacular views of the Roaring Fork River.

FACING PAGE: An open kitchen occupies one end of a continuous series of living spaces that run the length of the first floor. Here the emphasis on natural elements found throughout the house—sycamore cabinetwork, wooden floors and ceilings, and moss-stone chimney stacks—is contrasted with stainless-steel appliances and a bronze hearth surround. Interior design firm Leslie Jones & Associates gave the space Asian sensibilities with modern, minimalist furniture.

Photographs by Steve Hall, Hedrich Blessing Photography

"Consistency of material
and form creates a home
of true repose."

—Tom Beeby

TOP LEFT: A centrally located library also serves as a light well. Shelf placement and sycamore paneling are dictated by an established four-inch module. The core of the house, the space also opens outward to views of the Roaring Fork River beyond the living room.

BOTTOM LEFT: In the master bathroom, rich materials are integrated into a uniform surface, with a stainless-steel dado separating an upper zone with sycamore panels and bronze-clad windows from a lower zone of travertine. A flat mirror reinforces the master bathroom's planar qualities.

FACING PAGE TOP LEFT: Adopting the four-inch module used throughout the house, the staircase is clad entirely in sycamore paneling, which changes direction to distinguish a wainscot zone beneath the bronze handrail from the wall zone above. Handmade bronze railings conform to the contours of the hand.

FACING PAGE TOP RIGHT: Set into a native-stone chimney piece, the fireplace surround is forged from a single folded panel of bronze. The adjacent placement of a traditional Asian chair restates a larger theme of rustic simplicity in the company of precise construction.

FACING PAGE BOTTOM: Matching fireplaces in the kitchen and living area bracket a continuous living space faced on one side by bronze-clad windows that stretch from floor to ceiling. These, together with the open-slat decking on the covered patio beyond, dissolve the boundary between inside and outside, a strategy common to both traditional Asian and modern styles of architecture. This continuity with natural surroundings emphasizes this house as a retreat from the city.

Photographs by Steve Hall, Hedrich Blessing Photography

"Complementary elements from varying sources can be blended to create an evocative whole."

—Tom Beeby

TOP RIGHT: Reused Southern yellow pine floors run through an open vista along the house's central axis, which is reinforced by a stair landing that makes a covered entry just inside the front door. The fixtures and furniture conform to the Georgian character of the architecture.

BOTTOM RIGHT: Doors are located in the corners of the dining room to hold circulation to its edges, allowing the fireplace and dining table to reinforce the room's central axis. Paneling beneath the windows is pushed slightly forward to emphasize these as freestanding tabernacles. Georgian details and furnishings give the room a simple, formal character.

FACING PAGE: The house combines the formal elements of a mansion—such as the hierarchical arrangement and pure Palladian detailing of this central section—with the domestic character of a New England house, evident in the adjacent clapboard siding and dormer windows. The house's tripartite plan and elegant detailing recall the Hammond-Harwood House in Annapolis, Maryland, designed by William Buckland and constructed in 1774.
Photographs by Judith Bromley

No stranger to swinging a hammer or carrying bricks, Michael E. Breseman spent his boyhood years working alongside his father in residential construction. This early exposure to home building and remodeling inspired his career path. Michael earned a degree in architecture from IIT and has since become a sought-after designer on the North Shore, opening his namesake firm doors in 1994. His training emphasized the pure modernist approach of Mies van der Rohe, of "less is more" fame. Michael applies this profound axiom combined with timeless principles of proportion, balance, and massing to influence the exceptional detailing of his authentic traditional architecture.

Michael creates new homes and artful renovations for those living in prestigious Lake Forest, a suburb known for its exemplary David Adler architecture dotting the treed Lake Michigan shoreline. He was commissioned to renovate the Kearsy Coates Reed House, a 25,000-square-foot residence considered the epitome of David Adler's eclecticism. Michael designed multiple additions including a five-car garage, pool house, and pool conservatory and renovated the service wing adhering to historic preservation guidelines to remain consistent with the home's Georgian style. The signature theme of a new or renovated home designed by MEB Architects is comfortable, modern, 21st-century living grounded by timeless traditional architecture.

"Classical architecture done well can be the new modern—becoming new and refreshing only by the honest use of forms from the past."

—Michael E. Breseman

MICHAEL E. BRESEMAN ARCHITECTS, LTD.

"By designing an entry in human scale, a sense of delight is revealed and made more powerful as one steps inside the grand space."

—Michael E. Breseman

LEFT & FACING PAGE: To create a new French Country manor steeped in European roots, we designed the home with proper materials including authentic stucco on concrete block, Ludowici clay tile, and reclaimed barn wood. We had five antique fireplace hearths and mantels imported from France to bring historical beauty to the interior structure. The owners wanted to feel the French countryside in every detail. Based on our design concepts, artisans handcrafted the main door in warm wood with custom ironwork insets and a side entry door with ornate wrought iron mullions framed by a protective wood archway and lead-coated copper roof.

PREVIOUS PAGES: The exterior of the home should not be unified by the collection of its elements but by the binding force of the architectural style. We designed a new English Country home with subtle Tudor influence featuring twin gables and two-story bay windows with vertical fretwork. The sweeping conjoined gables provide drama to the massing of this home while the detailing of the bays gives harmony to the design. The classic residence reflects authentic European style and proportion.

Photographs by Michael E. Breseman and Justine N. Runvik

"The design process is a journey best served by pausing to reflect."

—Michael E. Breseman

LEFT: We transformed a 1980s home overlooking Lake Michigan into a French Country manor with a steeply pitched main gable, side tower, and portico. The new stucco façade with stone quoins creates authenticity, yet relates well to the existing brickwork of the original structure. We accented the windows with "Adler" blue-painted shutters and a warm, cedar shake roof, which allows the home to coexist beautifully in its wooded lakefront setting.
Photograph by Michael E. Breseman and Justine N. Runvik

"The art of architecture is what you remove; an erased line can be more powerful than the one that's drawn."

—Michael E. Breseman

ABOVE & FACING PAGE: We design in an array of styles and genres, but the details make the home come to life with authenticity. Cut limestone and artistic stonework customize with luxury and refined craftsmanship. The fluted arched entry and windows with stone muttons and mullions express the true English manor architectural style in correct proportion. Through appropriately specified materials, we defined a Tudor's addition with stacked casement windows, bracket work of stained white oak, and genuine clay tile roofing. To accentuate a formal French manor home, two distinctive dormers made of cut stone with characteristic European copper roofing were incorporated. As in life, we strive to strike a balance between the ornate and the simple.
Photographs by Michael E. Breseman and Justine N. Runvik, Thomas P. Pins

"I believe that God is in the details. He reveals himself with proper proportions, authentic materials, and finally by guiding the hand of the craftsman."

—Michael E. Breseman

ABOVE & FACING PAGE: Our designs require construction experts and seasoned craftsmen who fabricate and install Old World elements with extraordinary detailing, such as leaded glass windows with stone mullions. A screened porch utilizes reclaimed wood and stucco panels in perfect proportion and simplicity, while the portico features elliptical brick arches to create a walkway effect that leads to several garages. We work with builders, landscape architects, and local artisans in a team approach to design residences that exemplify their genre.

Photographs by Michael E. Breseman and Justine N. Runvik

Well versed in traditional and contemporary architectural styles, Elissa Morgante, AIA, and Fred Wilson, AIA, joined forces in 1987 to form Morgante Wilson Architects. The pair of Chicago's most sought-after architects designs primary and secondary homes in the heart of the city, on the North Shore, and atop Lake Michigan's most coveted beachfront properties. Their specialties include new home constructions, historic residential renovations, adaptive reuse, and innovative additions, not to mention numerous commercial projects. The duo's sensitive additions fit beautifully into historic districts, whether a small remodel or an extensive renovation; the architects can deftly deconstruct an old house and thoughtfully reconstruct it to seamlessly integrate into an established neighborhood.

Elissa and Fred complement one another. Fred is a big-picture thinker, while Elissa designs the fine details of an interior space. The firm has garnered professional awards for its sensitivity to historic areas, designing homes that appropriately integrate into longstanding communities for which the Chicago area is famous. MWA's team is comprised of 20 talented associates, and each commissioned project is a concerted effort; the architectural team collaborates with engineers, landscape architects, interior designers, and craftsmen to create some of the most remarkable private homes for discerning clientele.

"Our architecture is informed via travel, extensive reading, observing details, and attending design summits. We love to explore new environments and carefully study the nuances."

—Elissa Morgante

MORGANTE WILSON ARCHITECTS

RIGHT: We have a passion for designing homes that are traditional with a modern twist. The homeowners appreciated traditional architecture, yet they wanted to emphasize their more contemporary lifestyle. We designed a curved and flowing, casually elegant structure to express the relaxed way they live today. The home's backyard is bordered by a wood deck with Pennsylvania bluestone edging. Working closely with landscape architects, we arrived at the terraced design starting with the circular lawn; residents follow a handrail to the mid-level with geometric lap pool, then another flight of stairs leads down to the beach. We used reclaimed local tree trunks, cut and milled as columns, for the curvilinear crescent-shaped pergola. A practical stucco exterior weathers rough Lake Michigan winters.

PREVIOUS PAGES: The exterior elevation of a weekend home in Grand Beach, Michigan, takes advantage of its large site with a creek running through it, flowing over the beach and into Lake Michigan; the moving water carves an ever-changing landscape. The 7,000-square-foot second home was designed for longstanding clients who are very creative and great team players. The collaboration led to a more dynamic plan that unfolded harmoniously. We worked to maximize views by curving house sidewalls so every vantage point is unique. Residents enjoy a different perspective at every turn with changing foregrounds and long-distance views.

Photographs by Janet Mesic Mackie

"Each home should be a unique expression of the people who dwell within its walls."

—Fred Wilson

ABOVE: Four contemporary club chairs delineate the open-concept living room area with glass doors opening out to the lake as you step down to the sunroom. By integrating expansive windows and contiguous transoms to enjoy awe-inspiring views, we surrounded the terrace with contemporary glass panel railings for unobstructed vistas.

FACING PAGE: A large masonry wall of natural stone sourced from Arizona is visible from the exterior and rises inside the home to make the visual connection. Our curved walls are reiterated: The curved foyer can be seen from the curving balcony above the dining room. We suspended a light fixture from the second floor through the home's center for unity from top to bottom. From the kitchen perspective, you can look through the entire house when standing at the sink or see the gorgeous lake view. In the bathroom suite, we added an expansive wall of operational windows, so residents can enjoy breathtaking views and fresh air from the freestanding soaking tub.

Photographs by Janet Mesic Mackie

"Extensive renovations should pay homage to the historic neighborhood, but step it up for today's modern lifestyles."

—Elissa Morgante

RIGHT & FACING PAGE: A stately home in disrepair became an opportunity for massive renovations and a dream to be realized. The couple wanted their North Shore property to reflect the traditional center-hall American Colonial style, yet be a comfortable place where the active family could really live it up. Our renovation allowed room for more yard space, and we put on a sizeable addition that doubled the original home's square footage. We preserved two of the original structures: the main staircase and a single-story sunroom. A seamless renovation-addition project, the home looks as though it has always been there, never changing from its original structure.

Photographs by Janet Mesic Mackie

"A timeless home should evoke a sense of classicism, yet clearly integrate modern elements."

—Fred Wilson

ABOVE: No longer a pure New England Colonial aesthetic, the North Shore home exhibits a more contemporary attitude. An office tower right off the second-floor master bedroom gives the residents necessary privacy to conduct business and enjoy a bird's-eye view. The tower was designed directly above the original screened porch structure.

FACING PAGE: The interior spaces have a sense of continuity, showcasing traditional elements in the dining room, butler's kitchen, screened-in porch, and out to the European-inspired garden. We also designed the underground gymnasium, the first of its kind in the community. Working in collaboration with the city's strict zoning board and engineers to dig deep below the main basement, the basketball court features 18-foot ceilings and hardwood flooring for a year-round family recreation center.

Photographs by Janet Mesic Mackie

Stanley Tigerman, FAIA, and Margaret McCurry, FAIA, create private residences that vary as much in form and presence as the people for whom they are created, but there is a consistency. The architecture's understated presence exudes simplicity. Precise lines, deft use of materials, and interesting spatial relationships engage all who enter Tigerman McCurry Architects' innovative structures. It is difficult to articulate their form of genius, but Stanley and Margaret have been creating veritable works of art for decades.

From the Holocaust Museum in Skokie to private residences across the globe, in the world of architecture people know and respect Stanley and Margaret's work. Stanley, a Yale grad, serves on advisory boards at Yale, Princeton, and the Art Institute of Chicago; he served as Director of the School of Architecture at the University of Illinois and co-founded ARCHEWORKS, an alternative, socially responsible venue for design education. Margaret earned her art history degree at Vassar and was awarded a Loeb Fellowship for graduate studies at Harvard. Working independently, Stanley and Margaret design expressive dwellings throughout Chicago, across the country, and internationally, creating a legacy of timeless structures. Their alternative concepts and groundbreaking approaches have set a new standard for architects the world over.

"Great American architecture has a linkage to the past, a heritage that runs through the work. Even new designs should have a memory about them."

—Margaret McCurry

TIGERMAN MCCURRY ARCHITECTS

"A house should reflect the uniqueness of its residents. As a project evolves and the architect-owner relationship grows, we can express this aspect more fully."

—Margaret McCurry

LEFT & FACING PAGE: I created a concept for the interior spaces of the home in response to the family's desire for a practical, interactive layout that is also ecologically responsible. First-floor rooms are interconnected and trimmed in quartered American white oak. Limestone flooring resists dirt while conducting radiant heat. Above the two-story, cross axial atrium, a skylight floods the area with soft light. The double-height great room with its Fond du Lac stone fireplace is the focal point for family gatherings.

PREVIOUS PAGES: "The Orchards" residence is clad in white corrugated metal with low-E glass windows in cadmium yellow frames. I designed the 7,800-square-foot country home for a 30-acre site in rural Michigan. Its "whitewashed" Midwestern vernacular makes reference to common gable-roofed barns, conical silos, and slatted corn cribs. The geothermal system uses the ground temperature to heat and cool the house as part of an environmentally sensitive design. A cottage is linked to the main residence via the pool complex; the unique estate lies amid nature trails, wetlands, and an apple orchard.
Photographs by Steve Hall, Hedrich Blessing Photography

"Successful designs integrate seamlessly with nature. The site essentially determines how the house should live on the land."

—Margaret McCurry

RIGHT & FACING PAGE: I designed the contemporary, southwestern Michigan house as a serene country retreat with sweeping views through framed windows in bedrooms and baths, open lofts and connectivity throughout. An abundance of light enters the space, yet sun screens shade the interior for energy efficiency. Private gardens, orchards, and the native environment can be appreciated from every angle. This innovative homestead will live for generations.

Photographs by Steve Hall, Hedrich Blessing Photography

"Challenges of site, historic neighborhoods, and city restrictions for development give rise to fresh and creative architectural solutions."

—Margaret McCurry

ABOVE & FACING PAGE: I strive to create an inventive synthesis of modern classicism and the regional vernacular in my work. The "Double Low House" was designed to comfortably inhabit an established North Shore community. I wanted it to have a uniquely informal attitude to suit the family's lifestyle, yet meld with the neighborhood. The site's rear yard had a magnificent vista, so my design needed to optimize those views. Reverse gables hide myriad rooms with the perception, especially frontally, of only a few. Through strategic design, we were able to situate the generous 7,000-square-foot home on the small suburban lot within the Floor Area Ratio (FAR) Zoning guidelines set by the city.
Photographs by Steve Hall, Hedrich Blessing Photography

"Eclectic, visionary architecture provides an opportunity to explore alternatives and articulate them with purpose through built form."

—Stanley Tigerman

ABOVE & FACING PAGE: "Suburban Village" is unlike any single-family home ever created. The design is multifaceted, displaying different geometric shapes and post-modern elements within one cohesive whole. Stanley designed the residence for a mature couple with grown children; the program required a one-bedroom house, with library, living and dining rooms, kitchen, and separate guest quarters for visiting children and grandchildren. Built on a flat site with a cluster of large-scale trees at its western edge, the home was lined with clerestory windows to bring the outdoors in. He specified a wood frame, clad in stucco, with a base of limestone and varying roof forms covered in standing-seam zinc. Stanley's design incorporated wood windows, and the main "street" was paved in natural limestone. A swimming pool with changing rooms and cabana was also integrated into the contemporary complex for a complete villa lifestyle. Stanley designed the custom rug to whimsically reflect the plan of the residence.

Photographs by Bruce Van Inwegan

"A dream home becomes reality when talented craftsmen join forces with top architects and interior designers in total collaboration."

—Michael Wujcik

elements of structure

Everyone knows Chicago for its broad range of residential architecture styles: charming bungalows, historic Lincoln Park brownstones, Frank Lloyd Wright-inspired residences, prestigious North Shore estates, sprawling suburban residences, vintage condos, and elite penthouses on the luxurious Gold Coast. The city is rich in diverse ethnic neighborhoods, exciting urban life, and thriving surrounding communities. Since 1993, Skokie-based general contractor and residential builder Michael Wujcik has been commissioned to create exclusive historical restorations, new custom homes, condominium build-outs, additions, and renovation projects throughout the greater Chicagoland area.

Michael is committed to the company mission of building the highest quality residences utilizing experienced craftsmen and Old World artisans from his hand-picked carpentry team. Every member of the Wujcik Construction Group, from administrators to construction superintendants, possesses the same degree of integrity in maintaining constant communication with key architects and interior design professionals for the duration of each project. Michael's remarkable portfolio of award-winning work speaks for itself, and Chicagoans enjoy the fruits of his labor living in distinguished residences they are proud to call home.

Wujcik Construction Group, Inc.

"The secret to building a particular architectural style is to study historical precedent with the goal of authenticity."

—Michael Wujcik

RIGHT: The Zen experience begins the moment you see the authentic teahouse poised on a natural rock foundation; it appears to be floating in the manmade pond. We researched historic Japanese teahouse designs and followed tradition to create a backyard retreat gently integrated on the forested property. A glimpse inside the teahouse showcases its artful mahogany woodwork elements including floors, walls, and shoji screens. Our year-long endeavor was inspiring as we created a proper ambience for residents to enjoy the four virtues of tea: harmony, respect, purity, and tranquility.

PREVIOUS PAGES: Marvin Herman & Associates designed the North Shore ranch-style home to have an eclectic architectural flavor. We built the home to feature exterior mahogany millwork, which is also reflected in the home's interior spaces.
Photographs courtesy of Wujcik Construction Group

"Precise execution of refined details throughout the home provides a feeling of order."

—Michael Wujcik

ABOVE: An ofuro, the traditional-style Japanese soaking tub, is made from hinoki, a type of cedar with a soothing lemon fragrance. Handcrafted wood shoji screens filter daylight for privacy, yet the gardens are in view for relaxing pleasure.

FACING PAGE: We built the loggia to separate the driveway and garage court from the outdoor terrace and swimming pool area, yet unify the two spaces. Solid mahogany columns were fabricated by Parenti & Raffaelli, and hardwoods line the loggia ceiling beneath a slate roof.
Photographs courtesy of Wujcik Construction Group

"Through recurring use of materials, we deliberately connect the outdoor spaces to create an extension of the home."

—Michael Wujcik

ABOVE & FACING PAGE: The sprawling residence overlooks an 11-acre property. In keeping with the transitional architecture and neutral palette of the exterior façade, our millwork experts crafted the kitchen cabinetry of solid hickory with a characteristic prominent grain accented by durable granite countertops. We designed a custom plaster-finished stove hood for Old World elegance, completely lined with a stainless steel insert for ultimate functionality.
Photographs courtesy of Wujcik Construction Group

"The art of restoration is staying true to the genre both structurally and aesthetically."

—Michael Wujcik

ABOVE: We built a screened porch replete with a stone-faced fireplace, second-story terraces, and spacious stone patios for an indoor-outdoor experience to be enjoyed from spring through autumn.
Photograph courtesy of Wujcik Construction Group

FACING PAGE: We emphasized beam and arch elements for a newly constructed Lincoln Park home library designed by Wheeler Kearns Architects; glue-laminated, Douglas fir beams are structurally superior and were stain-finished on site. The fireplace facings, mantels, and custom-carved surrounds were created from hand-selected French Beauharnais limestone. Our artisans installed the rough-cut stone masonry veneers on the end walls made from Wisconsin's native Fond du Lac stone. Many of our interior stone elements are an extension of the home's exterior façade.
Photographs by Steve Hall, Hedrich Blessing Photography

"When the craftsmen control every aspect of the project—from design to installation—the outcome is flawless."

—Tom Stilp

ABOVE: Contrasts can make the strongest statements; we used travertine for the stairway's body, cherry on the side stringers, and forged iron balustrades—all set against a black walnut floor. The mixture of ferrous and non-ferrous elements makes a dramatic statement.

FACING PAGE: For a home with large, competing features, we wanted to make sure the stairway maintained its presence. We designed and constructed a massive bowed and flared bottom to offer the correct proportions. The starting newel posts and open riser add to a rustic, reclaimed feel and work well in a post-and-beam or cabin-style home.
Photographs courtesy of Arcways Stairways

"You should always be able to rely on the judgment of the professionals you're working with. Otherwise, you're working with the wrong professionals."

—Tom Stilp

ABOVE: We love a challenge; a complex design layout gave us just that. The 14-foot bottom mirrors the balcony treatment to balance the entryway at its centerline. Perfectly detailed with brass and verdigris, the custom forged iron railing flows through the midlanding space.

FACING PAGE: Trusting our expertise from 45 years of experience, the homeowner decided to go with gilded wood balusters as opposed to iron panels. From the marble floors to the imported Spanish balusters, the rich details play off one another to create a stunning, pristine foyer.
Photographs courtesy of Arcways Stairways

ABOVE: We wanted to keep the elements of a stairway historically faithful and at the same time aesthetically pleasing; we built oversized helical volute rail fittings at the base to achieve this. The complex project required precision and keen craftsmanship to get the perfect results.

FACING PAGE: To maintain a warm elegance, we juxtaposed carved wood newel post beginnings with iron panels and wood top rails. The custom forged iron balustrade with wood panelized side face creates a seamless visual flow that keeps with the graceful design.
Photographs courtesy of Arcways Stairways

"Seeing the intense amount of work—engineering, artistry, and craftsmanship—that goes into a stairway is something you never forget."

—Tom Stilp

ABOVE LEFT: Achieving a modern look without appearing too cold can be tricky, but we used wood and glass barrels to anchor the beginning of the stairway, offering warmth and personality. The use of sap maple contrasted with the glass panels adds to the effect.

ABOVE RIGHT: Precisely matching the grain and color of the sapele mahogany wood stair components is a highly involved process—but the results are well worth the investment. The bookmatched wood on the sides of the stairway nicely complements the modern interior.

FACING PAGE TOP: Complex and stunning, the design for integrating a companion elevator into a three-floor stacked stairway includes simple lines in a flat radius; the contrast was achieved through mixing black walnut and stained white oak.

FACING PAGE BOTTOM: The interior radius for the stairway's midpoint was extreme; we carefully crafted the tightness of the curves for precision. From the foyer, the stairs offer a lasting first impression with the flared and bowed base and helical barrel beginnings. Rich black walnut with a rubbed bronze forged iron finish adds to the striking appearance.

Photographs courtesy of Arcways Stairways

"I'm passionate about the renaissance of ornament in architecture and work to create genuine and permanent beauty in the built environment."

—Larry Zgoda

ABOVE: An octagon window illustrates my commitment to innovation in technique. I weld ornamental, forged steel components together to create a reinforcing armature that fortifies the matrix of colored glass pieces. I have an affinity for using arboreal and vegetal motifs in my designs. Green fracture-streamer glass modifies light with flakes of glass fused into the surface.

FACING PAGE: My original designs begin with hand-sketched line drawings and these pencil lines represent lead lines in the finished artwork. Inspired by the elegance of a brilliant sunrise, the double door's ornamental treatment of arcing lines suggests stylized sunrays. The composition features a variety of clear textured and amber iridescent glasses within a sphere. The dramatic architectural installation is illuminated with ambient indoor lighting, which imparts a golden glow.
Photographs by Richard Bruck

"The art of stained glass is color focused. I create fields of subtle tone accented with vibrant colors and prismatic hues."

—Larry Zgoda

RIGHT: The beacon window allows a softened exterior view with subtly textured, clear antique glass. Its stylized arboreal composition features aurora, gold-ruby, and copper-brown antique glasses punctuated with a checkerboard treatment of cut-polished square jewels. In sunlight, cut-polished jewels cast dramatic rainbow hues into the interior environment. Richly colored, spun glass rondels create a mosaic of polychromatic foliage.
Photograph by Ron Johnson

FACING PAGE: Over-the-door transoms showcase vibrant yellow circles of beveled crown glass. Crown glass is flashed with a thin layer of color over clear, so when the flashed side is beveled, the clear base is revealed. I am enthusiastic about architectural ornament, which is experiencing a true renaissance in today's culture and design vocabulary.
Photographs by Richard Bruck

"My compositions glorify qualities of light with prisms and other optical components of clear and colored glass. I work to create a kaleidoscope of color, pattern, and visual kinetics."

—Larry Zgoda

ABOVE: On exhibit in regional galleries, my freestanding, stained glass "Architonomous" art glass sculptures are inspired by architecture and allow for the exploration of new ornamental motifs. The term "Architonomous" is my amalgam of the words architectural and autonomous. Set into hardwood frames with weighted bases, these works offer the enjoyment of stained glass without custom installation or hanging.

FACING PAGE: Installed in a retro environment, I created Cascade using a prismatic approach; the ornamental window conveys the energy of a flowing waterfall. Clear chinchilla glass suggests water, with its soft and scintillating texture, richly flanked by copper-colored glass. The composition has staggered beveled squares and thick diamond shapes that capture natural rainbow effects when the sun shines through. Pink and blue glass pieces are symbolic of the sky, interspersed with cut-faceted jewels. Burgundy geometrics define the foreground, while brightly hued rondels accent each corner.

Photographs by Richard Bruck

"There are no hard and fast rules anymore. Like in fashion, choose tile that feels right and suits your personality and lifestyle."

—Mila Goldman

ABOVE & FACING PAGE: The homeowners wanted a clean and contemporary approach to their kitchen design concept but with unique pizzazz. Our soft taupe glass mosaic tile is understated, and the simple subway design adds interest without being busy or overwhelming.
Photographs by Peter Nilson

"Design trends may come and go, but high-quality handmade tiles are timeless."

—George Bañuelos

LEFT: The transitional master bath shower is lined with 12-inch-square natural limestone tile and features river pebble flooring in the same color family. Our glass mosaic accents of white, taupe, and chocolate brown add vertical interest to the limestone walls while creating the illusion of taller ceilings.
Photograph by Peter Nilson

FACING PAGE TOP: A powder room was designed with a juxtaposition of contemporary clean lines with interesting background textures. Straight lines of the vanity cabinet are complemented by rustic, tumbled slate mosaic tile. For the master bath in the same home, Gascogne Beige limestone walls and flooring were used. The subdued pattern exudes a serene feeling, much like an upscale hotel spa.
Photographs by Peter Nilson

FACING PAGE BOTTOM LEFT: The half-bath concept was inspired by elegant, bronze-finish porcelain fixtures. We created the custom vine design back wall, composed of glass mosaic tile and bronze-toned mirror pieces for a unique metallic sheen.
Photograph by Peter Nilson

FACING PAGE BOTTOM RIGHT: The homeowners wanted a fun bathroom for their young child, yet with a traditional look that wouldn't become outdated. Fresh white, handmade ceramic tile walls have a horizontal band of marble micromosaics in muted grey, ivory, and black tones; pure white handmade tile floors are interspersed with thin strips of the same neutral pattern reiterating the design element. Interior design by 2DesignGroup. Installation by McHugh Homes.
Photograph by Pov Corriveau

"Whether choosing colorful ceramic, lustrous glass, burnished metal, recycled leather, cement textures, or natural stone, trust your instincts and go for it."

—Lisa Bañuelos

ABOVE: The homeowners wanted to update their bathroom and visually open up the space. We chose harmonious natural materials for a tranquil and soothing retreat. The spacious glass-enclosed shower is lined with Positano glass mosaics complemented by a dramatic Black Sumatra river pebble floor; natural slate tile flooring throughout the room possesses enduring strength and eco-friendly appeal. Interior design by Foster Hill Design.
Photograph by Scott Steward Photography

FACING PAGE TOP: Kitchen cabinetry takes on a totally different look depending on the tile selection. Handmade, hand-glazed ceramic tiles have one-of-a-kind definition and subtle interest. Our American-made handcrafted bricks are slightly elongated for a modern twist on traditional crackled subway tiles providing a simple and clean backsplash.
Photograph by Peter Nilson

FACING PAGE BOTTOM: Rustic, handmade tiles laid on a diagonal with an ornately carved border and custom mural over the stove epitomize European flair. We combined cream, warm coffee, and espresso tones to create an inviting Old World look. Interior design by Gridala Design.
Photograph by Peter Nilson

BUILDERS IRONWORKS, INC.

Crete, Illinois

"Anything is possible with iron as the artistic medium."

—Rick Wories

ABOVE & FACING PAGE: Ironwork is an age-old art that has broad appeal; because it has such a great aesthetic, people sometimes feel intimidated by the prospect of commissioning a design for their home. It's more accessible than people think. While hand-forging every element would indeed slide the project into the cost-prohibitive category, my team and I have great resources that allow us to obtain countless iron components that are produced in volume by hand. We then piece them into custom, site-specific creations. I work with architects, designers, and homeowners to determine the best style for the project, work through sketches and shop drawings, and then provide a physical sample so that everybody knows exactly what the detailing and finish of the final piece will look like. *Photographs by Richard Allen*

"Custom ironwork is the 'jewelry' of a home. It has an alluring quality and leaves a lasting impression."

—Rick Wories

ABOVE: From a detailed shop drawing or something as simple as a magazine clipping, we have the ability to evolve an idea and execute it with precision. Some people prefer an ornate design while others are drawn to a clean-lined motif; the ultimate design should reflect the people who commission us, because it's about their personal style, not ours.

FACING PAGE: The architecture of a home is fundamentally and aesthetically important, but it's ornamental ironwork that often makes the first impression. Whether iron is transformed into elegant driveway gates or a dramatic staircase, it becomes an undeniable focal point. And because you can't hide imperfections in metal, it's critical that the base metal, decorative finishes, and overall craftsmanship are of superior quality. The more difficult and custom the work, the fewer the qualified craftsmen. We've been in the industry for more than two decades, and our portfolio of high-end work speaks for itself—even the most complex of designs is well within our reach.
Photographs by Richard Allen

"The discovery process should reveal people's needs, wants, personalities, and lifestyles."

—Stephanie Wohlner

elements of design

Some may call it a certain edge, yin and yang, an interesting mélange, or eclecticism, but Stephanie Wohlner's interior design style exhibits her love for the process of translating ideas into nuanced design. Stephanie has a passion for putting select antique pieces, contemporary furnishings, and fine art together in perfect juxtaposition that can be felt the moment one enters the room. Her strong sense of scale and proportion coupled with impeccable good taste has attracted opportunities to create timeless elegant interiors throughout Chicago, the elite North Shore, as well as Florida and New York.

Stephanie studied interior design at Chicago's Harrington School of Design after years as a children's special education teacher. Her patience and listening skills were honed, and today she reads clients so well that her signature environments reflect a desired lifestyle while truly contributing to the residents' wellbeing. Her design style captures an inviting beauty and real functionality, which has become her hallmark. She allows the home's architecture to speak to her, which very often inspires her designs. Wall and floor colors are kept consistent for a unifying flow, then she creates on the "blank canvas" using a light and dark mix of fabrics, furniture shapes, textures, and splashes of color. Sophisticated yet comfortable with fresh appeal, Stephanie's interiors are meant to be fully lived in.

STEPHANIE WOHLNER DESIGN

"Good design identifies personal taste, and then reinterprets it using a mix of elements."

—Stephanie Wohlner

ABOVE & FACING PAGE: Dark brown floors with putty-colored walls make the perfect backdrop for an eclectic mix of furnishings and recycled treasures. The owner's original Dakota Jackson card table ensemble boasts newly upholstered chairs. I transformed the awkward bedroom window into an asset framed by luxurious bedroom draperies and damask headboard. The chaise became an alluring retreat, while the mirrored quatrefoil armoire creates an edgy tension to the room, reflecting the outdoor garden. The large-scale chinoiserie coffee table and antique spindle-leg chair command attention in a living room that lacked architectural definition. One bold contemporary art piece ties the whole look together.

PREVIOUS PAGES: Contemporary art was the impetus behind a tailored family room design. By adding new windows in the 1970s-era home, natural light opens up the space; automated bamboo blinds easily darken the room for television viewing. The ottoman was originally a tufted leather piece; I reworked it, adding new legs to create clean lines, and covered the piece with Clarence House silk velvet in a zebra pattern. Print accent pillows, wicker chairs, and a unique sculptural lamp create visual interest.

Photographs by Tony Soluri Photography

"Interior design takes form when influenced by the home's architecture and aesthetic."

—Stephanie Wohlner

LEFT & FACING PAGE: To stay true to the blue-grey Nantucket clapboard house and its architectural genre, I used an eclectic approach and exciting contemporary twists to give a new interpretation, still respecting tradition. Crisp white cabinets and dark hardwood flooring finishes provide contrast, while brilliant artwork punctuates the space. My sense of appropriate scale and proportion along with room-delineating columns and a redesigned fireplace mantel bring a bright and clean, yet familiar traditional feeling to the home. Architecture by Stuart Cohen and Julie Hacker.

Photographs by Jon Miller, Hedrich Blessing Photography

"Yin and yang elements combine beautifully in a space."

—Stephanie Wohlner

ABOVE & FACING PAGE: All of my creative interiors tend to be quiet and peaceful environments, but with a few dark elements and interesting shapes to create tension. Refinished oak plank floors reflect the home's rich history. I layered the space starting with white built-in cabinetry and restored the home's original carved mantel; dark wooden antique chairs add sharp contrast, and wonderful wicker textures enrich the bath and bedroom spaces. We designed a built-in bar with its oval mirrored window as a new architectural detail that blends with the home's aesthetic and serves as a useful piece when entertaining.
Photographs by Jon Miller, Hedrich Blessing Photography

"Layered color and texture with artful lighting creates inviting warmth."

—Stephanie Wohlner

LEFT & FACING PAGE: I layered an Astor Street residence overlooking Lake Michigan with color and texture to emulate the shore, muted sky, and blue-hued water. Silk velvet Christian Liaigre dining chairs, subtle monochromatic bed linens, and caramel-colored antique leather club chairs from Paris bring lavish softness and warmth to the space. The apartment's traditional character features painted and wood-paneled walls, a vintage fireplace, and architectural details that harmonize with the modern art collection, Rose Tarlow sofas, and Holly Hunt walnut table. I sourced a chandelier with blue-green metalwork to mimic nature's palette; Rose Tarlow wallcoverings add a sea mist effect.

Photographs by Jan Mackee

"A new interior can have a sense of history with the right architectural built-ins and appointments."

—Stephanie Wohlner

ABOVE & FACING PAGE: My design for a new construction has traditional architectural details that make the home feel established. We incorporated mouldings, pine cabinetry, dark hardwood floors, and painted built-ins, and then mixed in textures and patterns. Vintage pillows, patterned rugs, and red accents enliven the rooms, while the checkered kitchen floor, bamboo window treatments, and leopard touches add an edge and connect with the dark flooring throughout the home. The dining room's Venetian glass chandelier from Donghia adds drama and glamour. A Fortuny silk chandelier in the bedroom exudes formal elegance, but the clean lines of the bed and book bench are crisp and contemporary.
Photographs by Linda Oyama Bryan

"The kitchen is the social core of the home. It needs to be visually interesting, warm, inviting, and above all, functional."

—Jean Stoffer

ABOVE & FACING PAGE: We strive to create classic kitchens with a fresh twist. Our simple, yet elegant look integrates architectural elements found elsewhere in the home. In the remodeled kitchen we added classic crown mouldings, several windows for a sparkling interplay of light, and an arched cooking alcove to reference the home's architectural aesthetic. Textured ceramic tile has a watercolor glaze that is visually interesting in its subtlety. Ebonized wood and polished calacatta marble runs counterpoint to white built-in cabinetry, while the modernity of a fully integrated stainless steel counter and sink juxtapose nicely with the warmth of traditional cabinetry. *Photographs by John Stoffer*

"The visual elements of a home's architecture can become inspiration for kitchen design."

—Jean Stoffer

ABOVE & FACING PAGE: The residence's historic Spanish architecture and a client's love of Mexico influenced my colorful, layered design. Soltiel floor tile was laid in an interesting pattern, while mesquite wood was carved for unique window lentils; many artifacts and decorative objects were collected to bring the ambience and vitality of Mexico into the space. Rustic wrought iron light fixtures, a magnificent walnut island countertop, hammered copper sinks, and turquoise glazed ceramic tiles blend to form an exciting Mexican-Spanish vibe. Architectural elements include built-in niches and stone-faced alcoves to define work and storage areas with panache.

Photographs by John Stoffer

"I enjoy applying classic design in a modern context."

—Jean Stoffer

RIGHT & FACING PAGE: We designed the kitchen of an 1872 Victorian jewel to be architecturally in sync with the home. The vernacular is typically imbued with dark woods and heavy ornamentation, but we used a more winsome approach of pared-down decorative details and lighter finishes, while keeping the same proportions and forms that resonate with the style. We found an antique wood cupboard with float glass doors and combined it with a custom wood range hood that was made to look like the same vintage. The turned legs of the island reference Victorian farm tables of old, but provide modern function by maintaining a height perfect for food preparation. A classic sink stand belies the sleek European dishwasher hiding behind the cabinetry. We have mastered the fine art of seamlessly integrating modern lifestyle kitchens and their technology with the vintage homes that host them.

Photographs by John Stoffer

"A feeling of simplicity and serenity is created by restrained and balanced design."

—Jean Stoffer

ABOVE & FACING PAGE: The classic 1920s-era Craftsman home has rectilinear form and symmetrical style. In keeping with its clean lines, simple white recessed panel cabinetry builds toward the center of the wall and climaxes with the architectural mantel range hood. We installed green polished granite countertops and coordinating backsplash tiles to bring a sense of harmony and calm to the work space. Contemporary-shaped alabaster pendant lighting adds 21st-century zing. Unique beveled mirror tiles were specially made for a horizontal feature on the backslash, inspired by the home's original beveled mirror art glass windows. The residents call it their kitchen bling.
Photographs by Mark Samu

ATELIER LAPCHI

"The perfect carpet expresses who we are and what we love: the colors, textures, and patterns that we find engaging and inspiring."

—Kerry Smith

ABOVE: Lapchi hand weaves carpets of exceptional beauty and ecological integrity. Lanolin-rich Himalayan wools and fine silks are dyed, spun, carded, woven, and finished entirely by the hands of Nepali artisans. These beautiful natural materials are tinted with eco-friendly dyes and require no harsh chemicals or finishes that might injure the breathtaking beauty of the Kathmandu valley or its people. While preserving an ancient art form, we also support GoodWeave, which means that our carpets are artful expressions of child-free, fair labor practice.
Photograph by Michael Jones

FACING PAGE: We have developed an extensive library of designs that can be customized in color, fiber, scale, pile height, and finish. It is rewarding to collaborate with interior designers and their clients to realize a vision—or to develop one—though many people find their perfect rug in the abundant variety of our showroom. It's all about line, form, and color. The Lapchi pattern library reflects a wide span of influence—echoes from thousands of years ago and provocative contemporary abstractions alike—and each motif has a story to tell. It's this level of thought and detail that defines all of our rugs, whether custom or tailor made from our collection.
Photograph by Nathan Kirkman

"Partnering with GoodWeave is part of our ongoing commitment to make each carpet an aesthetically special and socially responsible choice."

—Kerry Smith

ABOVE LEFT: Based on a French Deco silk in the African style, Chevron celebrates its exotic parentage by spiraling sensuously over the carpet surface. Its undulating movement creates a pattern that adapts easily to all furniture groupings and possibilities.

ABOVE RIGHT: An essay in mark making, Etched recalls the painstaking artistic technique wielded by master artists Rembrandt and Van Dyke and turns it into a new kind of luxury surface for the art of living. The simple repeating element creates a rhythmic surface of sophisticated flexibility.

FACING PAGE: Like deep space images seen though the Hubble telescope, Nebulous speaks of patterns that have no solid form but possess a moody presence, mystery, and elegance. As spatially evocative and abstract as a contemporary painting, Nebulous is fine art for the floor.
Photographs by Michael Jones

TOP: "Satori" is the moment of sudden enlightenment in Zen practice. Our Satori rug epitomizes the international interests and passions of the 18th-century enlightened view of the world. Its blossom-filled tendrils capture the cross-cultural fusion of East and West and the peaceful garden of the enlightened mind.

MIDDLE: Arrowroot echoes the fabled furnishings of Ming Dynasty China, where refined artistic connoisseurship was at its peak. The rug's spiraling vines and broad clustered leaves invite the eye to wander along its slender stalks.

BOTTOM: A lyrical trellis of leaves, tendrils, and dew-frosted pomegranates, Thalia pays homage to the nature-inspired visions of the Arts-and-Crafts movement and Japan's floating world. Celebrating the gentle beauty of silhouetted shapes and naturalistic details, Thalia is simple, timeless, and elegant.

FACING PAGE: Emerging from prewar Europe, the pattern of Meadow is at the cusp of traditional representation and geometric modernity. Bold shapes bloom across the carpet surface, looking at once naive and sophisticated, playful and restrained.
Photographs by Michael Jones

BILL BRUSS DESIGN

"Before designing an interior,
I get to know the homeowners
by sharing some wine,
conversation, and an exchange
of ideas. Artwork, furniture,
and accessories should reflect
their unique personalities."

—Bill Bruss

ABOVE: The Haberdasher Square Lofts condo owners wanted a slick metallic and industrial-looking kitchen with hints of blue as seen throughout their residence. We integrated stainless steel appliances and easy-care metallic gloss thermofoil cabinetry to achieve an urban high-tech style. The counter backsplash and toe kick boasts gleaming Italian glass tile by Sicis from the Iridium Mosaic Collection. A trio of cobalt blue pendant lights illuminates the sleek cooktop.
Photograph courtesy of Bill Bruss Design

FACING PAGE: We combined a cool mix of contemporary and traditional elements in the compact sitting area just off the kitchen space, featuring a hand-laid, broken mosaic fireplace surround set against neutral grey walls. Eclectic chrome and copper lighting fixtures complement forms in the abstract artwork. Accessories have unique character sourced from travels around the world, tying the room together. All room décor is from our haute lifestyle store, Design Inc.
Photograph by Kennedy Photography

"Open floorplans still need boundaries to define the space, taking into consideration size, scale, and traffic flow."

—Bill Bruss

LEFT: A high-rise dwelling with city views needed a quiet atmosphere with clean and simple lines. I placed modern sofas in an L-shape to create conversational seating, while deep purple mohair pillows soften the contemporary arrangement. A Christian Liaigre dining table complemented by chairs from the Holly Hunt collection centers the space. I selected an uber-chic Italian chandelier with faceted jewels to cast a subtle glow above for a traditional concept with contemporary flair. By finishing the room with the homeowner's oversized painting from Mexico, we created high-impact drama. The blonde wood-paneled media wall and finger-jointed limestone fireplace chimney further define the flowing condo space.
Photographs courtesy of Bill Bruss Design

FACING PAGE: Chrome yellow leather club chairs pop against the warm grey walls, creating a cozy fireside vignette. I designed the mosaic fireplace surround using an enduring materials palette of uba tuba, light grey, and absolute black granite trimmed with white oak millwork. Rich suede accent pillows echo the passionate red hues of the abstract painting.
Photograph by Kennedy Photography

"Reflecting the beauty of nature, organic materials work best to form the inspired aesthetic."

—Bill Bruss

TOP RIGHT: Recessed ceiling details define the Park Ridge home's open plan with a crisp, contemporary feel. For an eclectic touch, we integrated a carved marble fireplace reminiscent of classic French Country-style residences. Rich mahogany and warm woods lend a look of timelessness; coordinating pocket doors conceal audiovisual equipment.

MIDDLE & BOTTOM RIGHT: I renovated a cottage kitchen by opening all the adjacent walls and adding a central work island to create a roundabout traffic flow ideal for family entertaining. Rich wood tones and natural stone punctuated by the homeowners' favorite Tiffany-inspired stained glass light fixture exude an inviting ambience. We converted the 1930s-era home into a 21st-century space with a vintage vibe for the owners' casual summer lifestyle. The living room, kitchen, and dining room are united through common elements: stone and wood. Extra stone flooring was used in the fireplace surround to visually connect the space for a year-round experience.

FACING PAGE: My bathroom remodels are often inspired by nature. Stonework in monochromatic sandy beach colors, smooth river rock details, and eclectic granite varieties bring the outdoors in. Whether a rustic cottage look for a Wisconsin vacation home or a clean-lined spa in a private home on the Indiana dunes, complete gutting allows us to start from scratch. By incorporating extra storage cabinetry, a walk-in shower, and benches wrapping the Jacuzzi tub, old bathroom spaces are transformed into refreshing places free of clutter.

Photographs courtesy of Bill Bruss Design

"Illumination is an art form. Authentic designs, detailed craftsmanship, and high quality materials are the marks of a masterpiece."

—James Neumann

ABOVE LEFT: Fine-chiseled details and hand-polished Bohemian crystals make our recreated Louis XVI sconces indistinguishable from the original. We cast the reproduction sconce in precise detail, using an exquisite 18th-century antique fixture as our model. The original fixture held candles and was not hollowed, so we discreetly wired our new, authentically made sconce from the outside.

ABOVE RIGHT: Our beaded plume sconce has an air of elegance, dating back to the 1920s. Hundreds of individually faceted, polished crystals were hand-wired to the 23-inch frame. We were inspired by an original fixture salvaged from the legendary Jacques Restaurant on Chicago's Michigan Avenue, made more beautiful with fully cut, high-quality crystals instead of cut-glass beads from the period. The resplendent sconces cast a brilliant light.

FACING PAGE: Our warehouse holds a vast collection of vintage and fine antique lighting fixtures sourced primarily from Europe. Founded during the 1920s by metalsmith Armin Neumann, our second-generation lighting shop specializes in creating meticulous reproductions of antique fixtures and new custom lighting designs. Reminiscent of a classic French Louis XV design, the multifaceted, bronze hanging lantern was hand-wrought by our cadre of experienced artisans.
Photographs by Bower Corwin Photography

"Antique lighting lends a rich sense of history and timeless beauty to a room, transforming the ambience into something very special."

—Paul Jurkschat

LEFT: We discovered a rare antique Wedgwood chandelier circa 1890 on an excursion to France. Cast from solid brass, the exquisite boudoir lighting fixture features classical Wedgwood pale blue cameos with graceful female figures. Because it was in pristine condition, we only needed to electrify the petite fixture, bringing it into the 21st century.
Photograph by Bower Corwin Photography

FACING PAGE: Our impressive Renaissance Revival chandelier has a Florentine gold finish with oval, turquoise medallion accents. The dramatic 19th-century antique fixture was selected from our collection by the interior designer for a private residence. We often restore timeworn chandeliers to their original splendor, or modify existing finishes to work with the design concept and homeowners' personal style. Interior appointments by Lawrence Boeder Interior Design.
Photograph by Tony Soluri Photography

RIGHT: We designed and fabricated a pair of dramatic eight-foot-tall Art Deco torchières for a homeowner with a passion for the period. Made of brass with finely cast details and a polished-and-satin chrome finish, the streamlined pieces flank the home's main entrance. Opaline globes emit a soft, luminous wash of light; upper halves lift up for convenient bulb replacement.
Photograph by Bower Corwin Photography

FACING PAGE: We manufactured four-foot-tall lanterns to grace the Beaux-Arts façade of a luxury Gold Coast high-rise. Based on a Paris landmark hotel lantern, our creative metalwork team forged an elegant scrollwork design out of malleable brass. The non-corrosive medium has superior strength for enduring quality, and our ebonized finish contrasts the French limestone exterior. Well-supported with triple mountings, the lanterns will withstand blustery weather for years to come. Glass panels are satin etched for a soft, opaque glow.
Photograph courtesy of New Metal Crafts

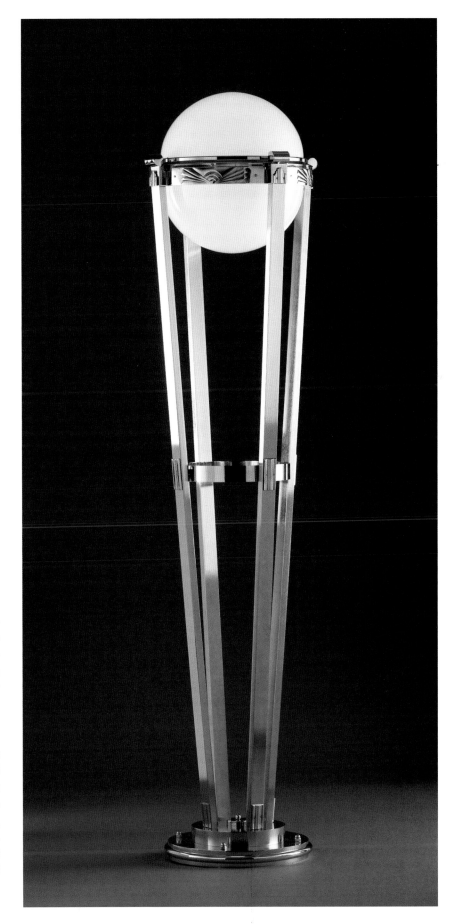

"Non-traditional surfaces are ideal for original murals, whether realism or fantasy."

—Paula Clayton

ABOVE: We decorated the interior wall with an extremely naturalistic landscape of woodland plants, towering trees, and a single cream-colored unicorn, so well-rendered that they seem real. The paint has the sparkling shimmer of mica flakes that intensify the glowing sunlight for a truly magical environment.

FACING PAGE: Every surface is a blank canvas, if primed and prepared properly. From concrete floors to ceilings, walls to clapboard siding, there lies an opportunity for painting a work of art. In a screened porch garden room, we used the vivid, offbeat style of artist Gustav Klimt to create a happy surprise, merging it with a classic mural inspired by the ancient Roman fresco painting *Livia's Garden*. The colorful hand-painted floor is sealed with a clear topcoat to resist wear.
Photographs courtesy of Signature Mural & Finish

"Painting murals and faux finishes melds art, trade, and craft."

—Debby Spertus

ABOVE: We transformed plain walls into a day at Avalon Beach, the homeowners' favorite vacation spot. Our sandy dune leads to the shoreline replete with seagulls, colorful umbrellas, sunbathers, and a wooden boat. Family photos and postcards were reference points for the bathroom painting. We designed the seascape so the full scene is reflected in the mirror and towels can hang in the foreground without obstructing the ocean view.

FACING PAGE: We have a passion for designing murals that delight the senses. Abstract patterns and textures, enchanted rainbows and fairies, a nurturing tree, or bold starlit stripes: our murals and faux finishes create an atmospheric quality. Adding energy to any room, murals can be sophisticated, cheerful, serene, or unexpected. We translate the homeowners' desires by creating their dreams using a variety of painting techniques.
Photographs courtesy of Signature Mural & Finish

"Inspiration can come from a feeling, a color scheme, or a definite theme."

—Debby Spertus

RIGHT: Picturesque Tuscan hillsides in a powder room were painted in the traditional palette of pale gold, burnt umber, and dark green tones.

FACING PAGE TOP: The waterfall and lush green landscape brings British Colonial style to the dining room. Trompe l'oeil fools the eye into thinking the scene is three-dimensional; we used the ancient technique involving realistic imagery to create an optical illusion. The architectural pillar is real, but the stone archways and balustrades are faux painted. We also lined the arches with gold hologram foil for a prismatic touch. Hidden from view, a greyhound portrait beneath formal urns honors the residents' beloved pet.

FACING PAGE BOTTOM: We enjoy working with multiple faux techniques and decorative products. Venetian plaster, stenciling, wood graining, gold leaf, concrete staining, and individually designed freehand murals are all within our repertoire. Experts in applying innovative products such as JaDecor wallcovering and Aurastone architectural coatings, we create finishes that mimic textural stone and polished marble countertops.

Photographs courtesy of Signature Mural & Finish

"The process of integrating a garden into a space is complex, but the result is a feeling of utter simplicity and beauty."

—Scott Byron

living the elements

One of the foremost landscape architects, native Chicagoan Scott Byron has carried his passion into the backyards of suburban residences, urban courtyards, and high-rise terraces for more than three decades. Scott Byron & Company focuses on residential landscape design from Illinois to Michigan to Georgia and the Bahamas—but has also been commissioned for notable commercial projects: seven public gardens in the Chicago Botanic Gardens and the landmark Water Tower and Pumping Station on Michigan Avenue, where pedestrians can enjoy the beauty of nature in the heart of the city.

Scott connects the outdoor site with its architecture in one harmonious whole. This holistic design aesthetic is evident in his seamlessly designed private gardens. Underlying each design is a thoughtful site analysis and solution, articulated by plantings. Scott says, "I am not a gardener, but I am a landscape architect who creates solutions using plant life." Plantings add interesting textures, colors, and definition to a space. He often creates "outdoor rooms," backyard havens for reading or enjoying nature. Some of Scott's signature spaces integrate sculptures that rise amid flowers complemented by relaxing fountain sounds to mimic the flow of brooks and streams. Expressing himself as a landscape architect, visual beauty is paramount, but Scott's garden designs are a true sensory experience.

SCOTT BYRON & COMPANY

"People should experience the whole space—the site, architecture, and garden as one."

—Scott Byron

ABOVE & FACING PAGE: An axial garden created depth where it was nonexistent. We created a feeling of great space on a narrow suburban lot through an allée of trees and formal boxwood hedges; the yard is anchored by the white painted house with complementary fencing. The space becomes an outdoor room where the porch and garden coexist. We installed a gazing ball fountain with a stainless steel vessel—water bubbles up the center and washes down with subtle sounds drawing people from the porch deeper into the garden. We sourced the unique fountain, which was made by an English sculptor, especially for the garden.

PREVIOUS PAGES: Our formal garden idea was executed through geometry of design using trees, textural grass, and plant shapes to create an illusory sense of depth. We designed the long, narrow parcel of land to appear as if it goes on and on into natural woodlands beyond.
Photographs by Tony Soluri Photography

"Good landscape design grasps the vision and provides a solution using the right tools, plants, sun, and sky to support the dream."

—Scott Byron

RIGHT: The challenge was to create an "outdoor room" environment for an open terrace that had no definition. When residents step onto the rooftop for dining or relaxing, the extraordinary city and lake views are unobstructed and the intimate garden feeling is evident. We designed and installed custom planters lined with boxwoods, evergreen trees, and vines; the low-profile landscape has a canopy of flowering crabapple trees for contrasting height and punctuation. Planted with colorful flowers to reflect spring, summer, and fall seasons, the sophisticated rooftop garden can be enjoyed year-round.

Photograph by Tony Soluri Photography

"Successful landscape design is the creative expression of a solution. Artful gardens reflect the site and its surrounding architecture."

—Scott Byron

ABOVE & FACING PAGE: We designed a contemporary urban garden on a small backyard lot, typical of homes on the near North Side. It was a blank canvas. The entrance is a traditional, lush landscape with a natural stone walkway that invites you in; a gentle turn to the right brings you further into the yard looking down over a manicured park setting. The raised sitting area is perfect for cooking outdoors and dining alfresco. We built a polished black granite plinth that spills water into a rill running the perimeter of the house to emulate soothing stream sounds. This unique water feature cleverly masks stressful street noise.
Photographs by Tony Soluri Photography

"Plantings support the design solution with defining shapes, textures, colors, and fragrance."

—Scott Byron

ABOVE & FACING PAGE: Residents enter through a series of hemlocks to arrive at the secret garden, designed for reading and meditation. The homeowners wanted a contemporary sculpture garden in their backyard, so we created two levels with varying textures for visual interest. A curved pathway of smooth polished stones appears like a flowing river; the sculptural figure "floats" on the winding river of rocks. Stepping stones unite the two levels and also lead to the swimming pool with patios.
Photographs by Tony Soluri Photography

"The melding of art with nature transports the viewer to another place, offering a spiritual experience."

—Scott Byron

ABOVE: We designed a classical European-inspired garden to complement the resident's private art collection. The curvilinear layout of the lawn creates added depth of field in the space. A stone bench rests at one end for quiet contemplation and an ideal view of the uplifting bronze nude sculptures worshipping the sun.

FACING PAGE TOP: An oxidized, abstract steel sculpture emerges from the densely planted flower beds becoming the focal point of the garden; our design features mature pines as the towering backdrop. When walking through the foliage, strollers naturally come upon the sculptural elements, meant purely for visual enjoyment.

FACING PAGE BOTTOM: We installed rectangular stone slabs to form a spirit bridge that symbolically protects the garden from uninvited energies. People walk over the bridge and enter another level of the garden. The landscape design starts with a dream; we simply reinterpret the dream using our tools.
Photographs by Tony Soluri Photography

PLATINUM POOLCARE AQUATECH, LTD.

Wheeling, Illinois

"All aspects of the design project should be examined. We dive deeply into people's lifestyle needs and preferences to create a highly personalized aesthetic."

—James D. Atlas

ABOVE: Connecting the outdoors to the indoors, the dramatic resort-style pool features a rock grotto and tunnel that leads the swimmer to a walk-up sauna lined with handmade imported tiles from Wales. Cave paintings and creatively crafted stalactites hang from its ceilings for an authentic look.

FACING PAGE: As the perfect complement to an uber-contemporary glass home, we designed a simple geometric-shaped pool to fit flawlessly into the tight urban space. We created volume by utilizing several elevation changes to incorporate the raised spa, water feature, and swimming pool.
Photographs courtesy of Outvision Photography

"Pools should fit seamlessly into the environment and emphasize the indoor-outdoor connection."

—James D. Atlas

RIGHT: Riders of the stone-textured and epoxy-sealed concrete slide pass by custom fire features as they plunge rapidly into the pool. Our custom design blends into its naturally wooded acreage and unites the outdoor living experience with the indoor pool house. Flagstone deck areas, natural stone coping, and boulder accents create a serene oasis complete with water features in the backyard for private sunbathing, swimming, and entertaining. Natural stone, copper pipes, efficient heating, pumps, and filtration equipment help to preserve the lifespan of the pool and are kind to the environment.

Photograph courtesy of Outvision Photography

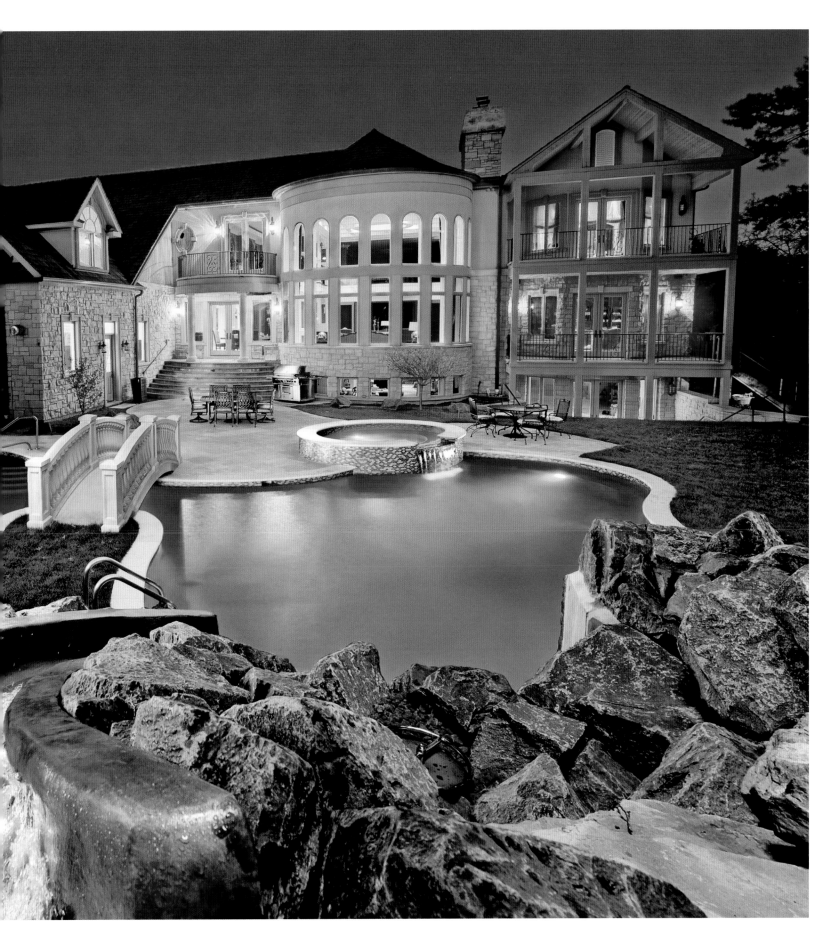

RIGHT: The elliptical-shaped indoor pool takes on an ocean blue glow when illuminated at night. Underwater lighting is an art form, and we are adept at planning, designing, and creating special effects that reflect the homeowner's taste. We integrated eco-friendly principles and superior technical systems to provide both form and function.

FACING PAGE: We were commissioned to create freeform outdoor pools that showcase beautiful perspectives with varying levels of several bodies of water. Behind the scenes, our designs reveal engineering innovations, security features, and hydraulics with superior structural solutions and equipment for the ultimate swimming experience. One pool's interior coating was custom blended to achieve a Caribbean turquoise color for a mesmerizing lagoon look. Ornamental gas-powered fire bowls with electronic ignitions have red glass effects to look like molten rock when burning.

Photographs courtesy of Linda Oyama Bryan

"A custom pool should be the exclamation point of a residence and a true reflection of the homeowner's sense of style."

—Terry Smith

ABOVE LEFT: The signature cantilevered seashell design is actually a swim-through entrance to the indoor pool from the connecting tunnel and cave. This theatrical element was hand sculpted and structurally made of the same fiberglass material used in fabricating the hull of a yacht. Its custom lining is an iridescent finish to resemble mother-of-pearl, and the textural, faux-coral ceramic tile covers the shell's exterior for a natural effect. The eye-catching, fantasy shell uses extremely complex technology.

ABOVE RIGHT: Our overall design of the indoor pool was based on a more formal, sophisticated vision. The chiffon scarf is made of handmade tile imported from Wales, inlaid to form the blue and white nautical stripe design flowing down the pool stairs. We commissioned an artisan to make elegant, curvilinear railings of brushed stainless steel to complement the pool.

FACING PAGE: Daylight floods the natatorium to showcase details from its one-of-a-kind seashell to the Italian travertine floors and automated windows.
Photographs courtesy of Linda Oyama Bryan

ABOVE: A Zen-inspired hydrotherapy pool suited to urban living also has an automatic cover that retracts under the coping of Pennsylvania bluestone. Both the pool and spa feature automatic pool covers with custom stone vanishing lid systems for safety and heat retention. Our efficient design allows the spa and pool to remain open in the colder fall and winter months without excessive energy bills.

Photograph courtesy of Outvision Photography

FACING PAGE TOP: We brought exotic flair and island inspiration to a sprawling suburban Northbrook home. Our 2,000-square-foot freeform swimming pool showcases native Wisconsin dolomitic limestone coping; the natural stone marries perfectly to the Turkish marble decking. A unique architectural bridge connects two sides of the pool. We had the bridge made of solid limestone for its aesthetic superiority and high quality that will surely stand the test of time.

Photograph courtesy of Outvision Photography

FACING PAGE BOTTOM: Fiber-optic lighting creates colorful illuminated effects; hidden flow jet fountains add a festive touch. We removed the home's original pool and created an impressive two-tiered rectangular swimming pool and spa with a natural Turkish travertine deck.

Photograph courtesy of Linda Oyama Bryan

Night Light, Inc., Landscape Illumination

Lombard, Illinois

"Exterior illumination should tell the landscape's story after dark by providing visual harmony between the key site and landscape elements."

—Dean MacMorris

ABOVE: Beautiful landscape illumination accentuates all of the home's charming exterior elements; most notably, the pergola, which is accented to entice people to come out and enjoy the space. The growing popularity of the "staycation" has made it increasingly more popular to bring outdoor features to life and give them prominence.

FACING PAGE: The motorcourt leads to a stately fountain that warmly glows to emphasize the rich details of the stonework, while the two trees beyond are bathed in cool uplighting that highlights their lush, healthy appearance. A series of coach lights along the drive guides the way to the entrance.
Photographs by Linda Oyama Bryan

"When nighttime falls, we use light as a paintbrush to enhance the beauty of the landscape while providing safety and security."

—Dean MacMorris

ABOVE: Moonlight and cool uplighting cast a crisp glow on landscape elements, creating a sense of space, while warm lighting suffuses the pergola. The melding of different tones and qualities of light unifies the landscape and affords a seamless transition between spaces.

FACING PAGE TOP & BOTTOM LEFT: The beautiful architecture is featured as part of the exterior composition by bringing out some of the key stone features and architectural elements. The home and landscape work in harmony to create a soft ambience of understated elegance.

FACING PAGE BOTTOM RIGHT: Connecting upper and lower spaces, the stone path has an informal, natural look. We echoed that feeling by downplaying the presence of lighting fixtures and specifying just enough light to make the walkway safe and beautiful.
Photographs by Linda Oyama Bryan

"The dark is as important as the light."

—Dean MacMorris

ABOVE: Working with the bronze fountain and existing entryway lights, we created drama by highlighting key architectural features, stonework details, and landscape elements; certain areas intentionally fall into shadow to create depth. A minimal quantity of carefully placed lighting fixtures produces the most natural and pleasing results.
Photograph by Norb Hansen

FACING PAGE TOP: A long serpentine driveway lined with staggered lampposts leads to the home, which is set on significant acreage. With cool lights on the landscape and warm lights on the architecture, the home stands as the clear focal point. When we're designing in a rural setting with limited ambient light, it's even more important than usual to illuminate selectively. Mystery and drama result when shadows are used to punctuate the highlights.
Photograph by Linda Oyama Bryan

FACING PAGE BOTTOM: Taking cues from the natural fieldstone façade, hand-hewn beams, wrought iron details, and stone patio, we created a very natural lighting scheme. The moonlit feeling comes from mercury vapor fixtures that are well-concealed in the trees. The space is lit well enough to keep guests from tripping but not so brightly that the warmth of candles is lost, creating a distinct outdoor experience.
Photographs by Norb Hansen

"We do for the earth what doctors do for the sick. Our patient is the land; restoring and maintaining the health of local plant communities is our top priority."

—Ron Bowen

ABOVE: Set in the Minneapolis suburb of Plymouth, a home landscape captures the allure of the Minnesota prairie in July. We created a garden—a concept that includes selected elements and careful design to accurately represent the natural prairie.
Photograph by Mike Evenocheck

FACING PAGE: With the nation's growing awareness of ecological concerns, companies have been moving toward presenting a strong image of compassion. When we worked with the leadership of the Lake Region Electric Cooperative in central Minnesota, they wanted to show their care and concern for indigenous preservation.
Photograph by Ron Bowen

> "Sincerity lies at the heart of the company. We started with genuine compassion, a logical idea, and the sturdiness of my old pick-up truck. And the sentiment has caught on—society notices the importance of what we've been doing for more than 30 years."
>
> —Ron Bowen

ABOVE LEFT: The prairie is a delicate ecosystem, storing soil and carbon to nurture flora and fauna. A midsummer scene demonstrates this as a monarch butterfly perches amongst butterfly milkweed, pink phlox, and black-eyed Susans.

ABOVE RIGHT: We gave charm to an open, rural residential site with careful orientation of each plant. Butterfly milkweed, vervain, and yellow coreopsis grow to the edge of the landowner's home.

FACING PAGE: My background has given me the tools to focus on the biological aspect of our work. Studies in forestry and a master's degree in landscape architecture have provided a technical base to work from and allow me to share the appeal of the land, in both function and form. A tallgrass prairie was restored for conservation and aesthetic purposes. The open countryside shows off prairie phlox and a variety of grasses in June.

Photographs by Ron Bowen

perspectives
ON DESIGN

CHICAGO TEAM

ASSOCIATE PUBLISHER: Heidi Nessa

GRAPHIC DESIGNER: Kendall Muellner

EDITOR: Anita M. Kasmar

PRODUCTION COORDINATOR: Drea Williams

HEADQUARTERS TEAM

PUBLISHER: Brian G. Carabet

PUBLISHER: John A. Shand

EXECUTIVE PUBLISHER: Phil Reavis

PUBLICATION & CIRCULATION MANAGER: Lauren B. Castelli

SENIOR GRAPHIC DESIGNER: Emily A. Kattan

GRAPHIC DESIGNER: Paul Strength

MANAGING EDITOR: Rosalie Z. Wilson

EDITOR: Jennifer Nelson

EDITOR: Sarah Tangney

EDITOR: Lindsey Wilson

MANAGING PRODUCTION COORDINATOR: Kristy Randall

PROJECT COORDINATOR: Laura Greenwood

TRAFFIC COORDINATOR: Katrina Autem

ADMINISTRATIVE MANAGER: Carol Kendall

CLIENT SUPPORT COORDINATOR: Amanda Mathers

PANACHE PARTNERS, LLC

CORPORATE HEADQUARTERS

1424 Gables Court

Plano, TX 75075

469.246.6060

www.panache.com

www.panachedesign.com

index

THE PANACHE COLLECTION

CREATING SPECTACULAR PUBLICATIONS FOR DISCERNING READERS

Dream Homes Series
An Exclusive Showcase of the Finest Architects, Designers and Builders

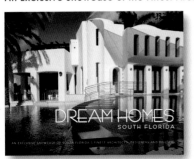

Carolinas
Chicago
Coastal California
Colorado
Deserts
Florida
Georgia
Los Angeles
Metro New York
Michigan
Minnesota
New England

New Jersey
Northern California
Ohio & Pennsylvania
Pacific Northwest
Philadelphia
South Florida
Southwest
Tennessee
Texas
Washington, D.C.

Spectacular Homes Series
An Exclusive Showcase of the Finest Interior Designers

California
Carolinas
Chicago
Colorado
Florida
Georgia
Heartland
London
Michigan
Minnesota
New England

Metro New York
Ohio & Pennsylvania
Pacific Northwest
Philadelphia
South Florida
Southwest
Tennessee
Texas
Toronto
Washington, D.C.
Western Canada

Perspectives on Design Series
Design Philosophies Expressed by Leading Professionals

California
Carolinas
Chicago
Colorado
Florida
Georgia
Great Lakes
Minnesota

New England
New York
Pacific Northwest
Southwest
Western Canada

Art of Celebration Series
The Making of a Gala

Chicago & the Greater Midwest
Georgia
New England
New York
Philadelphia
South Florida
Southern California
Southwest
Toronto
Washington, D.C.
Wine Country

Spectacular Wineries Series
A Captivating Tour of Established, Estate and Boutique Wineries

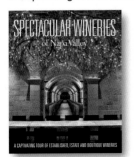

California's Central Coast
Napa Valley
New York
Sonoma County

Specialty Titles
The Finest in Unique Luxury Lifestyle Publications

Cloth and Culture: Couture Creations of Ruth E. Funk
Distinguished Inns of North America
Extraordinary Homes California
Geoffrey Bradfield Ex Arte
Into the Earth: A Wine Cave Renaissance
Spectacular Golf of Colorado
Spectacular Golf of Texas
Spectacular Hotels
Spectacular Restaurants of Texas
Visions of Design

City by Design Series
An Architectural Perspective

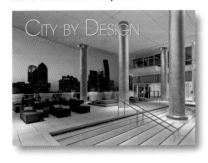

Atlanta
Charlotte
Chicago
Dallas
Denver
Orlando
Phoenix
San Francisco
Texas

PanacheDesign.com
Where the Design Industry's Finest Professionals Gather, Share, and Inspire

PanacheDesign.com overflows with innovative ideas from leading architects, builders, interior designers, and other specialists. A gallery of design photographs and library of advice-oriented articles are among the comprehensive site's offerings.

Panache Partners, LLC   1424 Gables Court   Plano, Texas 75075   469.246.6060   www.panache.com

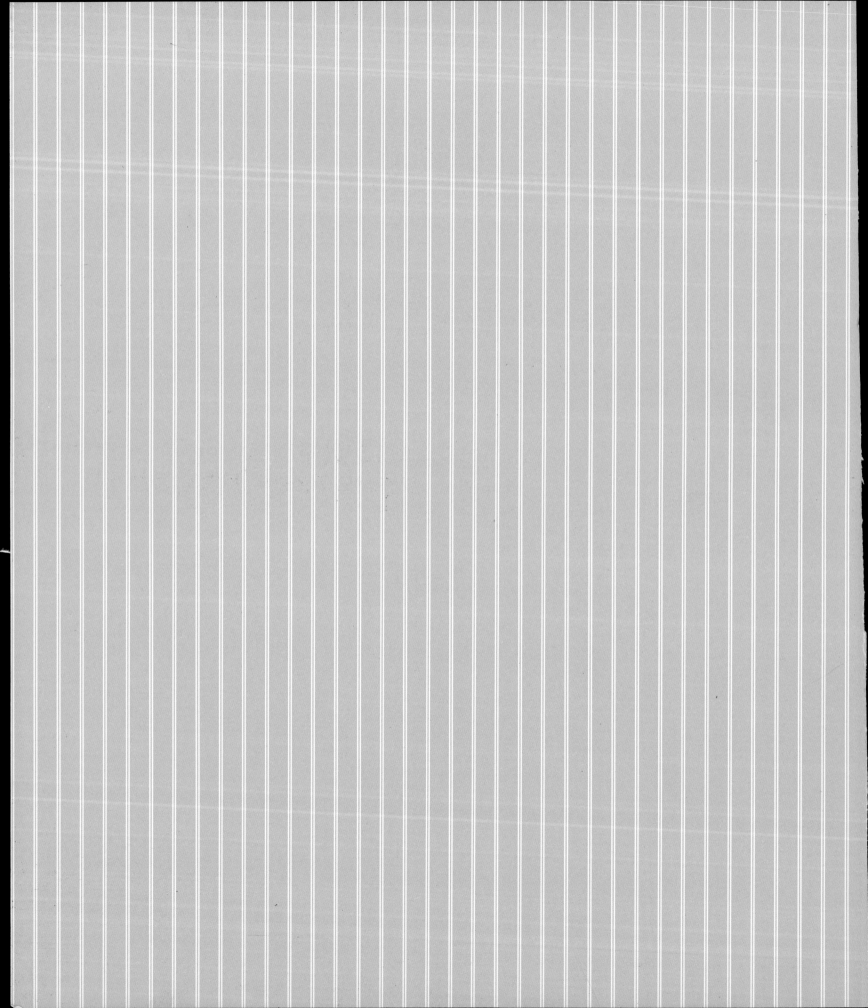